A Note From Rick Renner

I am on a personal quest to see a "revival of the Bible" so people can establish their lives on a firm foundation that will stand strong and endure the test as end-time storm winds begin to intensify.

In order to experience a revival of the Bible in your personal life, it is important to take time each day to read, receive, and apply its truths to your life. James tells us that if we will continue in the perfect law of liberty — refusing to be forgetful hearers, but determined to be doers — we will be blessed in our ways. As you watch or listen to the programs in this series and work through this corresponding study guide, I trust you will search the Scriptures and allow the Holy Spirit to help you hear something new from God's Word that applies specifically to your life. I encourage you to be a doer of the Word He reveals to you. Whatever the cost, I assure you — it will be worth it.

> Thy words were found, and I did eat them;
> and thy word was unto me the joy and rejoicing of mine heart:
> for I am called by thy name, O Lord God of hosts.
> — Jeremiah 15:16

Your brother and friend in Jesus Christ,

Rick Renner

Scripture quotations marked (*AMPC*) are taken from the *Amplified® Bible.* Copyright © 1954, 1958, 1962, 1964, 1965, 1987 by The Lockman Foundation. Used by permission. www.Lockman.org.

Scripture quotations marked (*NKJV*) are taken from the *New King James Version®*. Copyright © 1982 by Thomas Nelson. Used by permission. All rights reserved.

Scripture quotations marked (*NLT*) are taken from the Holy Bible, *New Living Translation*, copyright © 1996, 2004, 2015 by Tyndale House Foundation. Used by permission of Tyndale House Publishers, Inc., Carol Stream, Illinois 60188. All rights reserved.

Scripture quotations marked *RIV* are taken from *Renner Interpretive Version*. Copyright © 2021 by Rick Renner.

Scripture quotations marked (*TLB*) are taken from *The Living Bible* copyright © 1971. Used by permission of Tyndale House Publishers, Inc., Carol Stream, Illinois 60188. All rights reserved.

How To Overcome a Spirit of Fear and
How To Speak Faith to Yourself in Troubled Times

Copyright © 2023 by Rick Renner
1814 W. Tacoma St.
Broken Arrow, OK 74012-1406

Published by Rick Renner Ministries
www.renner.org

ISBN 13: 978-1-6675-0330-1

eBook ISBN 13: 978-1-6675-0331-8

All rights reserved. No portion of this book may be reproduced or transmitted in any form or by any means — electronic, mechanical, photocopy, recording, scanning, or other — except for brief quotations in critical reviews or articles, without the prior written permission of the Publisher.

How To Use This Study Guide

The lessons in this study guide correspond to *"How To Overcome a Spirit of Fear and How To Speak Faith to Yourself in Troubled Times" With Rick Renner* (Renner TV). Each lesson in this study guide covers a topic that is addressed during the program series, with questions and references supplied to draw you deeper into your own private study of the Scriptures on this subject.

To derive the most benefit from this study guide, consider the following:

First, watch or listen to the program prior to working through the corresponding lesson in this guide. (Programs can also be viewed at **renner.org** by clicking on the Media/Archives links or on our Renner Ministries YouTube channel.)

Second, take the time to look up the scriptures included in each lesson. Prayerfully consider their application to your own life.

Third, use a journal or notebook to make note of your answers to each lesson's Study Questions and Practical Application challenges.

Fourth, invest specific time in prayer and in the Word of God to consult with the Holy Spirit. Write down the scriptures or insights He reveals to you.

Finally, take action! Whatever the Lord tells you to do according to His Word, do it.

For added insights on this subject, it is recommended that you obtain Rick Renner's book *Life in the Combat Zone*. You may also select from Rick's other available resources by placing your order at **renner.org** or by calling 1-800-742-5593.

PART 1

TOPIC
How To Overcome a Spirit of Fear

SYNOPSIS

Fear — it's been around since the moment man disobeyed God in the Garden of Eden. Just as it caused Adam and Eve to run and hide from God then, it continues to cause people to run and hide today. Left unchecked, fear will stop us dead in our tracks, paralyzing us from any further progress or the advancement of God's Kingdom.

If any New Testament believer understood fear, it was Timothy. We know for certain that he was struggling with fear because Paul specifically wrote to him and said, "For God hath not given us the spirit of fear; but of power, and of love, and of a sound mind" (2 Timothy 1:7).

So, what insurmountable odds was Timothy facing at that time that caused Paul to make this bold declaration? Likewise, where was Paul, what was he dealing with, and what did he write and tell Timothy in his letter that we can apply in our own lives to overcome the spirit of fear?

The emphasis of this lesson:

When Rome declared war on all Christians in 64 AD, it was the result of Nero spreading fake news. His false charges brought persecution and great fear to the Church, including the believers in Ephesus where Timothy was pastoring. Paul addressed the issue of fear directly and reminded Timothy of his rich spiritual heritage. And by remembering God's faithfulness in the past, we, too, can stir up the gift of God that's in us and defeat the spirit of fear.

Timothy Wrote Paul for Help

The Bible includes two separate letters written by the apostle Paul to Timothy, a young man whom he fondly referred to as his spiritual son. Paul opened his second letter by saying:

> **Paul, an apostle of Jesus Christ by the will of God, according to the promise of life which is in Christ Jesus,**

> To Timothy, my dearly beloved son: Grace, mercy, and peace, from God the Father and Christ Jesus our Lord.
>
> I thank God, whom I serve from my forefathers with pure conscience, that without ceasing I have remembrance of thee in my prayers night and day;
>
> Greatly desiring to see thee, being mindful of thy tears, that I may be filled with joy.
>
> — 2 Timothy 1:1-4

These verses are simply jampacked with meaning, which we will carefully unpack throughout this lesson. But first, let's look at the word "tears" in verse 4. It is a form of the Greek word *dakry*. Here, it is used as plural, which indicates not just a single teardrop, but more than likely it describes *sobbing*.

It appears that Timothy, who was serving as the lead pastor of the church in Ephesus, had written a letter to Paul out of great desperation. In fact, the challenges he was facing were so overwhelming that most scholars say Paul's reference to "thy tears" indicates that the letter he received from Timothy was visibly stained from the young minister's weeping as he wrote the letter.

Essentially, Timothy poured his heart out to his mentor Paul, explaining everything he was going through and asking him for help and wisdom on what to do in the situations in which he found himself. As the pastor of the largest church in Asia, Timothy only had Paul whom he could turn to and confide in during such a crisis. Ironically, when Timothy wrote his letter, Paul was in a prison in Rome himself, accused of a crime he didn't commit. So what was going on in the world at the time of this writing? For the answer, we turn to First Century history.

Nero's Twisted Family Tree

For the record, Christianity was never a persecuted faith until the year 64 AD. The persecution we read about in the book of Acts, especially in the earlier years, were all religious persecutions. There was no official, governmental persecution against the Church until nearly 30 to 40 years after Pentecost. But in 64 AD, something very strange happened, and it took place under the rule of the Roman Emperor Nero.

To understand how Nero was wired, we must look over his family tree and get a snapshot of some of his relatives who were influential in his life. For example, his great-grandfather was Caesar Augustus — the same man who had an affair with Cleopatra, was a close friend of Herod the Great, and who declared that he was God.

When Caesar Augustus' reign came to an end, the throne went to Caesar's nephew and his adopted son Tiberias. History documents that Tiberias was a sexual pervert. In fact, he was so sexually twisted, that he eventually took up residence on the isle of Capri, which he called "The Orgy Island" or "The Pleasure Island." His intention was for orgies to take place on that island 24 hours a day. It was from this deviant place that Tiberius ruled the Roman Empire for 14 years. There was even a little town on the Sea of Galilee named Tiberius that was built in his honor.

On the isle of Capri with Tiberius was his nephew, Caligula. Caligula was mistreated sexually by his uncle and by the other men on the island, and when Tiberius died, Caligula came to power in his uncle's place. Sadly, he had been so mentally and sexually abused by his uncle for all those years that he brought all his twisted thinking and abuse to the throne with him. What would a man in his condition do if the power of the world was placed in his hands?

History tells us that Caligula, like his great uncle Caesar Augustus, also believed himself to be God. In Caligula's case, he believed and fashioned himself after the Greek god Kronos who was said to have eaten the babies of one of his sisters. So when Caligula's sister gave birth to twins, he ate them to prove that he was the equivalent of the god Kronos. This sick and twisted soul ruled Rome for four years.

When Caligula died, the throne went to his uncle, whose name was Claudius. Claudius married a woman named Agrippina, and Agrippina was the sister of Caligula. At some point during his life, Caligula had had an incestuous relationship with Agrippina, so she too had a measure of twisted abuse permeating her soul. She carried that perversion to the throne when she became the wife of Claudius, the emperor.

How does Agrippina fit into the scheme of things? It appears she had a son from a previous marriage. This son's name was Nero, and Agrippina wanted Nero to be the next Emperor of Rome. History reveals that to accomplish her desire, Agrippina fed her husband, Emperor Claudius, a bowl of poisonous mushrooms. Shortly after he died, she proclaimed that her son Nero was the new emperor of the Roman Empire.

Narcissism Drove Nero's Every Decision

When Nero ascended to the throne, he was only about 16 years of age. Can you remember what you were like at age 16? Can you imagine giving all the ruling power in the world to a 16-year-old? Even worse, can you envision telling him he was a god and could do anything he wanted and that nothing he did was wrong? Well, that's what Agrippina did with her son Nero, and she created a monster.

Nero quickly began to embrace the idea of his divinity and went to work eliminating anyone who disagreed with him. Two of the first people to go were his teachers Seneca the Younger and Lucius Annaeus. Their deaths were followed by the killing of certain members of the Roman Senate, and when Nero could no longer tolerate the nagging manipulation of his mother, he had Agrippina killed as well.

Finally, Nero seemed to be free to do anything he wanted or dreamed. Pride and arrogance oozed from his life, and he believed he was great at everything. For instance, he believed he was the greatest musician and actor that ever lived. Even though it was not permissible for emperors to perform, Nero ignored protocol and took to the stage to act and sing.

History tells us his singing was *horrific*, but no one dared to get up and leave while he was performing because if they did, they would be killed. There's actually record of a full-term pregnant woman who attended one of his concerts that gave birth to her baby during the performance because she was afraid to walk out.

In addition to his aspirations of performing, Nero also believed he was the greatest architect that ever lived. Consequently, he began to design himself a new home, which he called "The Golden Palace." It would be a house completely veneered in mother-of-pearl, which was then to be covered with gold leaf. Hence, it was called "The Golden Palace," and it was to be 300 acres in size.

But there was a problem. The location where Nero wanted to build his house was the most historic section of Rome, so when he went to the Roman Senate and requested to tear down the historic section of the city to build his palace, they told him no. Essentially, they said, "Nero, you may think you're God, but we're not going to let you tear down *our houses* so you can build your palace."

Of course, Nero wouldn't take no for an answer, so he went to a group of his servants in a village near his existing palace just outside of Rome and said, "I want you to go into the city of Rome and set a fire in the Circus Maximus stadium when the people are gone." They obeyed him, and the fire they set soon engulfed the entire city. By the time the blaze had gone out, the section where Nero wanted to build his palace was reduced to rubble. He could now construct the 300-acre home of his dreams.

Time passed, and rumors began circulating throughout the city of Rome that it was Nero who instigated the fire. The Roman Senate called him to stand trial for his actions with the possibility of execution if convicted. Immediately, his devious mind went to work, and while he was en route to the Senate, he conceived a diabolical idea — a scheme that would leave an indelible mark on history.

Nero's Performance Before the Senate Turned the Roman Empire Against Christians

When the day came and Nero finally stood before the Senate and they brought their charges against him, he gave his greatest performance of all time. "How could you think that *I*, Nero, would burn down my beloved city of Rome?" He cried. "I can tell you who did this because my spies have brought me information."

"Tell us," the Senate said, "Who burned down the city of Rome?"

"It was those Christians!" Nero snarled. "They're a new sect in our town, and they're the ones who burned down the city of Rome." Nero then brought five allegations against the Christians, which had some elements of truth but were overall untrue. Keep in mind a partial truth is a whole lie. You might say this was the beginning of *fake news*. If you think fake news is new to our lifetime, think again. The Bible says, "…Nothing under the sun is truly new" (Ecclesiastes 1:9 *NLT*).

Take, for another example, transgenderism. It's not new. History tells us that a person could only be a priestess in the cult of Cybele (Sibyl) in the ancient city of Smyrna if he started as a man. You had to go through a surgical procedure to have all your male anatomy removed, and you had to become a woman to become a priestess in the cult of Cybele/Sibyl. This means the First Century Church had to deal with transgenderism. Again, there's nothing new under the sun. Just as the Church was anointed to deal with sexual twistedness then, we are anointed to deal with it now.

Five False Charges Nero Brought Against Christians:

The first allegation Nero said was, "*Christians are lawbreakers.* They don't have permission to meet, yet they're meeting in underground secret meetings." To a degree, that was true, because people couldn't meet as a group unless they had the express approval of the emperor. Since Nero never gave his approval, every time Christians met together, they were breaking Roman law.

But they had to make a choice — a choice we, too, may have to make. "Do we obey the law of man, or do we obey the law of God?" The law of God clearly states we are not to forsake the assembling of ourselves together as believers (*see* Hebrews 10:25). Roman law said they could not meet. So, they had to decide which law they were going to obey, and they chose to obey the *higher* law — God's law. In doing so, they violated Roman law. In man's eyes, they were called lawbreakers, but in God's eyes, they were covenant keepers.

Second, Nero cited that in their underground, illegal meetings, *Christians are talking about another King and another Kingdom.* Of course, they were talking about Jesus and the Kingdom of God, but Nero made it sound like Christians were rebellious subverters of government. Doesn't that sound familiar to what some people are saying in our own time?

Third, Nero said, "*Christians are sexual perverts.* In their illegal gatherings, they practice something called, 'The love feast,'" he claimed. To understand just how ridiculous this accusation was, we have to look at Nero's life, who at that time was married to two men. Without question, he was as twisted sexually as one could be. So for him — a sexually perverted person — to accuse someone else of being sexually twisted, was ludicrous. Yet, he alleged that Christians were having orgies of the worst kind.

Nero's fourth allegation was that *Christians are cannibals*. He told the senate, "The leader of their sect, Jesus of Nazareth, said, 'Except you eat My flesh and drink My blood, you have no part in Me.' And in their illegal, underground meetings, they're eating flesh and drinking blood!" Of course, this was Holy Communion, but Nero was so effective with this charge that the Church had to fight rumors of cannibalism for the next 200 years. Again, *fake news* was at work.

Finally, Nero claimed that *Christians are the ones who burned down Rome.* He said, "I don't know how or why you think *I* burned down the city of Rome. Haven't you heard what these Christians have been saying on our streets? They've been standing on our corners preaching that in the future, a *huge fire* of judgment is going to come. We should have listened to them because they were giving us a clue that they were going to burn down the city of Rome."

By the time Nero was finished, he was so convincing that the Roman Senate believed him, and for the first time in history, in the year 64 AD, governmental persecution began against the Church in all the major cities of the Roman Empire. These included Rome, Alexandria, Antioch, and Ephesus. Where was Timothy? Timothy was in the city of Ephesus.

Rome's Persecution Placed Timothy in a Very Perilous Place

The church in Ephesus during the First Century was the biggest church in the world. It was estimated to have had about 100,000 members, and they were living in amazing revival. Paul had installed Timothy as the senior pastor over this thriving megachurch, but when the fires of persecution came, it began to reveal those who really were committed to Christ and who were not.

The truth is it's easy to serve the Lord when things are easy and it costs you absolutely nothing. However, when fiery trials come, it always reveals the true identity of people and our commitment to Christ. Of course we're not wishing fire on anyone. Nevertheless, whether we like it or not, fire comes at some point in all our lives. It can come to our relationships, our ministry, our business, our finances, or our health. This fire is not sent by God; it's from the enemy and the world system over which He presides.

When the fire of Roman persecution hit the church of Ephesus, Timothy, who had been enjoying being the pastor of the world's largest church, discovered that some of the people he thought would always be with him were just fair-weathered believers — including some believers that he had raised up to be leaders in his church. "Pastor, we never knew our faith was going to come to this," some of them must have cried. "But if we remain faithful to Christ, we're going to lose our lives."

From that moment forward, people began leaving the church. And now, whereas Timothy was pastoring the world's largest church, he was now pastoring the world's biggest church in decline. Additionally, because he was the pastor of the church in Ephesus, he was the most visible Christian in the entire city. He knew that at any moment, there could be a knock on his own door, and he could be arrested for his faith. He also realized if the Roman authorities could get their hands on him, they would make his death the most miserable of all to make him an example to the other believers of what would happen if they remained faithful to Christ.

A spirit of fear had begun to work viciously against Timothy, and at the time of the writing of Paul's second letter, Timothy had given place to that fearful spirit.

Paul Addressed Timothy's Issue of Fear Head-On

Having received Timothy's letter of desperation and seeing the parchment stained by his tears, Paul knew his spiritual son in the faith was in trouble. Under the inspiration of the Holy Spirit, Paul declared, "For God hath not given us the spirit of fear; but of power, and of love, and of a sound mind" (2 Timothy 1:7).

Fear is a spirit. That is exactly what the Bible says here. You can feel fear when it comes into the room. It is a spirit that brings fear, panic, dread, and terror with it. In fact, the Greek word for "fear" Paul uses here is a form of the word *deilia*, which means *timidity, fearfulness,* or *cowardice.* It describes *something that causes you to retreat* or *something that causes you to feel the need to protect yourself.* If fear has a hold of you, you're no longer advancing — you are *cowering, retreating,* and *going into hiding.*

A spirit of fear seeks to paralyze you, and when you're in ministry like Timothy was, it can totally inhibit your ability to function. It affects your ability to love others, to walk in power, and to have a sound mind. When a spirit of fear is operating in you, you don't think soundly. Instead, you think of everything bad that could possibly happen to you. It's as if your mind becomes a movie screen, and every imaginable negative scenario begins to play out before you — including things that could never happen.

As the leader of the church of Ephesus, Timothy became paralyzed. He was so hurt by the people whom he once trusted but were now walking out on him that he was having a hard time trusting others. It was difficult for him to walk in love as well as walk in the power of God because he had been seized by a spirit of fear.

We have been given power. Paul reminded Timothy that he had been given "power," which is the Greek word *dunamis*, a word you may have heard before. It is the same word used by Jesus in Acts 1:8 to describe the presence of the Holy Spirit that came to indwell believers on the Day of Pentecost. This word *dunamis* describes *explosive power* and is where we get the word *dynamite*. What you may not know is that *dunamis* is the very Greek word that was used to describe *a force of nature* — like a *hurricane*, a *tornado, or an earthquake*. It is also the same Greek word that was used to describe *the full might of the advancing Roman army*.

The use of this word lets us know that when the power of God is operating in you, you become like a *force of nature*. In other words, you are a spiritual *earthquake* that can shake things up or a dynamic spiritual *tornado* or *hurricane* that blows things out of the way. Furthermore, when God's power is operating in you, you're like *a one-man army* with the power to force back darkness. All this meaning is in the word *dunamis* (power).

The Spirit of God also provides us a sound mind. The phrase "sound mind" in Second Timothy 1:7 is taken from the Greek word *sophroneo*, which is a compound of the words *sodzo* and *phroneo*. The word *sodzo* means *to save* or *to deliver*, and the word *phroneo* carries the idea of a person's *intelligence* or *total frame of thinking* — including one's *emotions, rationale*, and *logic*. When compounded, these two words form *sophronismos* — translated here as "sound mind" — and it describes *a mind that has been delivered, rescued, revived, salvaged, and protected and is now safe and set free of all inhibitions*.

Taking into account the original Greek meaning of "sound mind," here is the *Renner Interpretive Version (RIV)* of Second Timothy 1:7:

> **God has not given you a spirit of fear, but of power and love — He has given you a mind that has been delivered, rescued, revived, salvaged, protected, and brought into a place of safety and security so that it is no longer affected by illogical, unfounded, and absurd thoughts.**

In Christ, We Are To Be Dominated by Life and Filled With His Grace and Peace

There's something important we don't want to miss in the opening verse of Paul's letter. He said, "Paul, an apostle of Jesus Christ by the will of God, according to the promise of life which is in Christ Jesus" (2 Timothy 1:1).

Notice the words "according to." They are a translation of the Greek word *kata*, which describes *something that is dominating, subjugating*, or *conquering*. Keep in mind, at that moment the Church — including Timothy — felt like it was being encumbered by a spirit of death on every hand. Yet, despite that, Paul, jumped out from the start and essentially declared, "…*I am dominated, conquered, and subjugated* by the promise of life that is in Christ Jesus." He began the epistle with a declaration that we are dominated by *life* — regardless of how much *death* is going on around us.

Then, in the next verse, Paul said, "To Timothy, my dearly beloved son: Grace, mercy, and peace, from God the Father and Christ Jesus our Lord" (2 Timothy 1:2).

It's interesting to note that when Paul wrote most of his epistles, he said, "Grace and peace be unto you." The reason he spoke this greeting is significant. It was not just a pleasant theological formula he concocted. On the contrary, when he said, "Grace and peace be unto you," he was speaking directly to both Greeks and Jews.

How do *Jews* greet each other? They say, "Peace" or "*Shalom.*"

How do *Greeks* greet each other? They say, "Grace, or "*Charis.*"

Therefore, when Paul said, "Grace and peace be unto you," in his epistles, in this one little phrase, he was wrapping his arms around the entire world! It was the equivalent of him saying…

"To all of you who are Greeks, I say, '*Grace* be unto you.'"

"To all of you who are Jews, I say, '*Peace* be unto you.'"

Saying, "Grace and peace be unto you," was also Paul's way of wrapping his arms around the Church, which is neither Jew nor Gentile, but one in Christ (*see* Galatians 3:28). In this one statement, he hugs all believers of all backgrounds. Of Paul's 13 letters, he used this same identical greeting 10 times.

There's Special *Mercy* for the Overwhelmed

Now, in Second Timothy 1:2 — as well as in First Timothy 1:2 and Titus 1:4 — he tucked the word *mercy* between grace and peace, and his reasoning for doing so is important. In Timothy's case, Paul was writing to a young man that was very overwhelmed by what he was encountering in life.

For Titus, the reason for including *mercy* between grace and peace was because Paul had left him on the isle of Crete *by himself*. In fact, when you read what Paul wrote to Titus, you get the impression that Paul basically abandoned him there with the purpose of completing everything Paul had left undone.

Who were the Cretans? Good question. Paul, in his not-so-politically correct way, said, "…The people of Crete are all liars, cruel animals, and lazy gluttons" (Titus 1:12 *NLT*). Ironically, this description came from a fellow Cretan! Paul was just repeating what had been said. History reveals that when the people of Crete celebrated weddings, they were known to take the former boyfriend of the bride, tie him to a team of horses, and drag him behind the wedding party until he died. That's the kind of people Timothy was left with — alone — on the island of Crete. It's no wonder that Titus was so overwhelmed by his assignment that when Paul wrote to him, he didn't just say, "Grace and peace be unto you, Titus." Rather, he added the word *mercy* as well.

Likewise, when Timothy was overwhelmed by a spirit of fear because of persecution, Paul tucked *mercy* between the grace and the peace. This tells us that if any of us are feeling overwhelmed by what we've been called to do, God inserts extra *mercy* between His grace and peace. When God's mercy works in our lives, it may manifest as a renewed sense of courage and inner toughness to make it to the next day. What a blessing God's mercy is!

Through Our Prayers, We Build Monuments and Memorials in God's Presence

Paul went on to say, "I thank God, whom I serve from my forefathers with pure conscience, that without ceasing I have remembrance of thee in my prayers night and day" (2 Timothy 1:3). Now, many just read right over this verse as simply a nice gesture made by Paul. But there is so much more in this verse than that, and it is found in understanding the meaning of the word "remembrance."

In Greek, the word "remembrance" is *mneia*, the ancient word for *a statue, a monument*, or *a memorial*. Hence, a more literal translation of the original Greek text of what Paul is saying here would be, "Timothy, I am building statues, monuments, and memorials of you in my prayers."

Another very clear use of this word *mneia* is in Acts 10:3 and 4 where an angel appeared to a devout, Roman officer named Cornelius who feared God. The Bible says that the angel told Cornelius, "…Thy prayers and thine alms are come up for a *memorial* before God" (v. 4). The word "memorial" is the very same word *mneia*. Cornelius' prayers and his giving to those in need were seen in Heaven as a statue, monument, or memorial in God's presence.

In Timothy's case, Paul basically told him, "Timothy, in my prayers, I'm building statues, monuments, and memorials of you in God's presence. So, everywhere God looks, He sees you. I'm stacking the throne room with statues, monuments, and memorials of all you've done to advance God's Kingdom."

Friend, never believe that your prayers are of little to no value. If all you can do is pray for others — PRAY! Every time you call a person's name in thanks to God, you're building a statue, a monument, or a memorial of that person in God's presence that is constantly before Him. Whenever you pray in faith or give money in faith, your words and gifts don't just vanish into thin air. If it's done in faith, it builds monuments and memorials in the annals of Heaven! God never forgets a prayer that is prayed or a gift that was given. That is the power of our prayers.

Timothy's Situation Wasn't as Bad as Paul's

When we come to Second Timothy 1:4, Paul told Timothy, "[I'm] Greatly desiring to see thee, being mindful of thy tears, that I may be filled with joy." Remember, at some point earlier, Timothy had written a letter to Paul expressing the dire situation he was in. Essentially, Timothy said something like, "Paul, you have no idea how I feel. I'm suffering here in Ephesus, and if you were here, you'd understand the traumatic events I'm going through. People I worked side by side with for years have walked out and abandoned me. I need you to help me, Paul. What am I to do?"

Where was Paul when he received Timothy's letter? If you remember, in the introduction we noted that he was in prison suffering for his faith. The irony here is that Timothy — the *free* man — is reaching out to Paul — the *bound* man — asking him for help. Isn't that how we usually react when we're all in trouble? We usually think that *our* situation is worse than everyone else's. That's how Timothy was feeling. Although Rome had begun a new wave of attacks against Christians, Timothy was still free to walk the streets of Ephesus, while Paul was in prison, bound and abandoned by everyone except God.

The reason Paul was in prison is that when this governmental persecution began after the Great Fire of Rome, Roman officers began rounding up Christians because Nero had falsely accused them of setting the city on fire. It was during this time that Christians began to be burned at the stake. The reason they were executed by fire is because according to Roman law, a criminal was to be killed according to the crime they committed. If a person was a thief, his hand was cut off. In this case, if a person was an arsonist, they were burned at the stake.

Paul was among the Christian leaders that were rounded up and charged as an arsonist. As he sat in prison, fake news was being spread all over the city of Rome. Back in those days, there weren't newspapers and TVs, so the current news stories were written on community walls for every passerby to read. "The chief arsonist that planned the fire of Rome has been captured and is in prison!" they said. Paul was a Roman citizen, so he was guaranteed to receive mail. He was aware of the false allegations that were circulating in the city about him, but he couldn't do a thing to defend himself.

Paul Reminded Timothy of His Rich, Spiritual Heritage

Timothy likely wanted some sympathy and comfort from his seasoned mentor, but that is not what he received. Yes, comfort and encouragement are helpful at times, but by the Spirit's discernment, Paul realized this was not the time for that. To tell Timothy that everything was going to be all right was not true. Instead, Paul told his spiritual son what he really needed to hear. It was time for Timothy to step forward as a man of faith, rather than retreat in fear.

Specifically, Paul said, "When I call to remembrance the unfeigned faith that is in thee, which dwelt first in thy grandmother Lois, and thy mother Eunice; and I am persuaded that in thee also" (2 Timothy 1:5). When Timothy heard these words from Paul, he may have thought, *Why are you talking to me about my grandmother and my mother? I'm the one in trouble. Please tell me something that will help me.*

Although Paul's words may seem strange, a closer look at the original Greek text reveals that he was telling Timothy something valuable. For instance, the word "dwelt" is the Greek word *enoikeo*, a compound of the words *en* and *oikos*. The word *en* means *in*, and the word *oikos* is the Greek word for a *house*. When compounded to form the word *enoikeo*, it means *to dwell in a house* and describes *a person who takes up residency in a house and enjoys a prosperous life there.* By using this word, Paul was telling Timothy that his grandmother and mother had a thriving faith that took up residency in each of them.

Paul also said they had an "unfeigned faith." The Greek word for "feigned" means *hypocrisy*, which is the same word that was used to describe *the masks that were worn by actors on the Roman and Greek stage.* In ancient times, if you were an actor on stage, you wore a mask. Interestingly, actors back then were considered to be the lower rung of society, because they would do and say anything for the applause of the people. They didn't mean a word they said. All they did was put on a new mask for whatever crowd they were in front of at that moment.

Is it any wonder that Jesus used this very word to describe the Pharisees? He called them *hypocrites* because they were always wearing masks and putting on a show for whomever they were standing in front of. This was the equivalent of Him saying, "I know who you guys are. You're just wearing a mask for the applause of the crowd. You don't mean a word you're saying. You're just putting on a show for the people that are watching."

When Paul told Timothy that his grandmother and mother had an "unfeigned faith," he was saying their faith was *authentic, real, and genuine* — not bogus or pretend. Then he added, "Your faith is the same kind, Timothy. It's genuine and real — not bogus or pretend. The kind of faith that took up residency in your mom and grandmother was passed on and is now thriving in you!"

Remembering God's Faithfulness Is a Powerful Weapon Against Fear

It's important to understand that from Timothy's vantage point, his future was very uncertain. With the dreadful news of Rome taking aim at Christians, a spirit of fear had taken hold of him, leaving him virtually paralyzed. To help his spiritual son break free from fear's clutches, Paul turned Timothy's attention away from the present and future and encouraged him to look back at his past.

The reason we often become immobilized by fear over our future is because we have forgotten the faithfulness of God in our past. That is what Paul was trying to communicate to Timothy. Basically, he said, "If you'll look at your past, Timothy, you'll see that God was faithful to your mother and your grandmother. They went through very difficult times as well, but God brought them through every situation they faced. And He will bring *you* through too."

Paul told Timothy, "Wherefore I put thee in remembrance that thou stir up the gift of God, which is in thee by the putting on of my hands" (2 Timothy 1:6). Notice the phrase "I put thee in remembrance." It is taken from the Greek word *anamimnesko*, a compound of the words *ana* and *mimnesko*. The word *ana* means *again* or *to repeat something*, and the word *mimnesko* means *to be reminded of something*, such as memories. When these two words are joined to form *anamimnesko*, it means *to regather* or *recollect memories*.

By using the word *anamimnesko*, Paul was telling Timothy, "I'm reminding you that God's faithfulness is a part of your family heritage. I'm hitting the rewind and replay button on your mind so that you'll remember your grandmother and mother both had a real faith, and God was faithful to them. He never let them down or let them fall through the cracks. He was always with them, and He will always be with you."

Paul then added, "…Stir up the gift of God, which is in thee by the putting on of my hands" (2 Timothy 1:6). Many of us hear this part of the verse and say, "Yes! That's what I need and that's what I want — for someone to lay hands on me." However, the Greek here actually says, "That *by your remembering them*, **you can stir up the gift of God** that is in you."

Your Memory Is a Tool To Stoke the Fire of the Flickering Embers of Your Faith

Clearly, receiving God's strength through the prayers of others is a great blessing. But what do you do if you're by yourself and there's no one to lay hands on you? How are you going to stir up the gift of the Holy Spirit in you? Like any fire that is dying out, in order to stir up the embers of your faith, you have to have a *poker*. In this passage, we learn that every one of us has a spiritual "poker," and it's called *memory*.

Paul's words to Timothy — and us — in Second Timothy 1:6 could be translated:

> **I am putting you in memory of all these things, so that by remembering them, you might stir up the gift of God that is in you….**

By remembering and remembering and remembering God's faithfulness to you in the past, you will stir up the gift of God that is in you. So, even if there is no one else to lay hands on you, you can choose to say, "I'm pressing pause on this fear, and I'm going to remember as many things as I can that God has ever done for me in the past." As you walk through one event after another event after another event, you'll realize what you're facing now probably isn't any worse than something you've already faced.

When work was scarce, your bank accounts were empty, and you had no idea how you would pay your bills, God brought you through. Or when you or your children were deathly sick and you saw no remedy in sight, God walked you through to recovery. Likewise, when your relationships came under attack and you felt you had no one to turn to, God's friendship became more real than ever, and He fixed what you thought was unfixable.

Rick said, "I could write a book about what has come against me the last two years of my life. If there was ever an opportunity to operate in a spirit of fear, believe me, I have had it. Through it all, I had to make a choice — *repeatedly* — to remember God's faithfulness to me in the past. You have to make that same choice. Are you going to focus on the fearful threats and gloom and doom that seem to loom overhead? Or are you going to fix your eyes on Jesus and remember His faithfulness to pull you out of every dilemma and bring you to where you are now?"

Remembering the faithfulness of God in your past is what *stirs up your faith* and strengthens you to face the future without fear.

Paul Talked to Himself While in Prison

Don't forget that Paul wrote his letter to Timothy while he was in prison. In other words, what he was telling Timothy to do, he had to do himself. Yet, instead of focusing on the fake news floating around the city of Rome and the fact that he was sentenced to death for a crime he didn't commit, he said:

> **...Nevertheless I am not ashamed: for I know whom I have believed, and am persuaded that he is able to keep that which I have committed unto him against that day.**
> — 2 Timothy 1:12

There are several key words in this verse that deserve our attention. The first is the word "ashamed." It is the Greek word *epaishunomai*, which means *to be disgraced, put to shame, embarrassed,* or *to be red-faced*. Despite everything that was being said about Paul, he was not disgraced or embarrassed. Even though he was in prison, he was not ashamed. Why? He said, "...For I know whom I have believed..." (2 Timothy 1:12).

In Greek, the phrase "I know" is a translation of the word *oida*, which means *to see, perceive, understand, or comprehend*. It describes *knowledge gained by personal experience* or *personal observation*. Paul had personally experienced the Person and power of Jesus Christ, and as a result, he said, "...[I] am persuaded that he is able..." (2 Timothy 1:12). The word "persuaded" here is the Greek word *peitho*, and it describes *one who is convinced, coaxed, or swayed from one opinion to the opinion held by another*. This is a person who has *absolute confidence* and is *convinced to the core* with *rock-solid certainty*.

The use of this word *peitho*, translated as "persuaded," tells us that while Paul was suffering in prison, he had moments when he was tempted to be fearful or to worry about what would happen, and because he had no one to talk to him or lay hands on him, he did a lot of self-talk. That is what this word *peitho* can describe — *self-persuasion*. With his own mouth, Paul talked to himself and walked himself out of fear and into a position of faith. When we're in trouble, we need to talk to ourselves and remind ourselves of who God is and what He's done in our lives. We have to push back against the devil's lies and turn a deaf ear to our emotions.

You must realize that no one's words are more powerful to you than your own. In fact, God's Word spoken in faith from your own mouth — over your life and against the enemy — has a greater impact than anything else this world has to offer!

Romans 10:17 says, "...Faith cometh by hearing, and hearing by the word of God." In the original Greek, this verse actually says, "...Faith comes by hearing and hearing and hearing and hearing...." Your head and your heart will believe what you repeatedly hear. If you're constantly speaking negatively about yourself and your situations, you're going to believe it, and it will become your reality. BUT if you use your mouth to begin speaking and speaking and speaking words of faith founded in Scripture, your mind and heart will believe it, and it will become your reality.

Friend, there comes a time for your spirit to tell your soul — and the enemy — to shut up! Paul came to this realization in prison and shared this game-changing principle with his young apprentice, Timothy. "Don't focus on your present problems," he said, "Or on the possible troubles awaiting you in the future. If you're afraid, you've forgotten God's faithfulness in the past. I'm hitting the rewind and replay buttons and recalling to your memory God's goodness to you in the past." It is by remembering and remembering and remembering the good deeds of the Lord that you stir up the gift of God that is in you.

Paul talked to himself in that dark, dank prison and coaxed and convinced himself that God was "...able to keep that which [he had] committed unto him against that day" (2 Timothy 1:12).

How God Enables Us To Partake of the Afflictions of the Gospel

Immediately after Paul put Timothy in remembrance of God's faithfulness, he told him, "Be not thou therefore ashamed of the testimony of our Lord, nor of me his prisoner: but be thou partaker of the afflictions of the gospel according to the power of God" (2 Timothy 1:8).

When Paul told Timothy not to be "ashamed," once again he used the Greek word *epaishunomai*, which is the same word he used for "ashamed" in verse 12. It means *to be disgraced, put to shame, embarrassed,* or *to be redfaced.* Apparently, Timothy was tempted to feel embarrassed and disgraced to be associated with Christ. Hence, Paul said, "Be not thou therefore ashamed," which in Greek is a strong prohibition meaning, "Stop feeling embarrassed and disgraced about your faith in Jesus, and stop it now!" Timothy was also admonished by Paul to stop being ashamed and embarrassed about his imprisonment.

Instead, Paul urged Timothy, "…Be thou [a] partaker of the afflictions of the gospel according to the power of God" (2 Timothy 1:8). We who have lived in America, have really not suffered great affliction for the sake of the Gospel. However, in the last few years, it appears as though we've entered a new age. Paul calls it the "last days," saying, "This know also, that in the *last days* perilous times shall come" (2 Timothy 3:1).

The word "last" here in Greek is *eschatos*, and it is a navigational term describing *the last port*. Essentially, Paul is talking about *the end of the age*, telling us, "When you've sailed to the very last port and you can sail no further, you will have come to *the very end of the age*. And perilous times will come." That is the territory in which we're living, and in that territory, we might have to deal with some afflictions for the Gospel.

If we do have to be partakers of the afflictions of the Gospel, Paul said we will do it "…according to the power of God" (2 Timothy 1:8). Once more, we see the words "according to," which are a translation of the Greek word *kata* — the same word we saw in Second Timothy 1:1. This word *kata* describes *a dominating force — something that dominates, conquers,* or *subjugates*. Here Paul is informing us that if we will take a stand for what's right and refuse to budge, even if it seems society is against us, something supernatural will take place. Paul says the power of God will show up and *kata* — begin to dominate us, conquer us, and subjugate us. In other words, God will come and join Himself to any person, or group of people, who is standing for truth and the Gospel and refusing to budge.

God's Power Is Our Sustaining Force

It is this divine display of God's power in believers who were suffering for their faith that nearly drove Nero crazy. History reveals that when he had Christians dipped in tar, tied to stakes in his backyard, and then set on fire, He would lean out of his balcony window waiting to hear them shriek in pain. But instead, he would hear them singing songs of praise while they burned. This is what nearly drove him crazy. The ancient writers said these Christian martyrs were "singing songs antiphonally unto God." Apparently, the power of God so consumed and dominated them in their final moments, that they were singing in tongues while they burned. They had overwhelming victory even in the fire, and they didn't feel it!

This same dominating, conquering power of God is available to all who choose to do what is right in any circumstance. His divine power is not just for believers suffering physical persecution. It is for those who stand firm and choose to do what's right in their marriage, their business, their ministry, their finances, their church, etc. Even if it creates a difficult situation and people don't like the righteous stance you've taken, God's power will show up and be your sustaining force.

Friend, if you've been unable to conquer a spirit of fear, you are dealing with a memory problem — you're forgetting about the goodness and mercy of God. If you're overwhelmed by what's in front of you, stop staring at the difficult circumstances and refocus your gaze on God's faithfulness in the past. Even if the trouble you're in is self-inflicted, Jesus — our Good Shepherd — is on the job and stands ready to reach down and pull you out of your mess. He did it before, and He will do it again.

You get to choose what you're thinking about and talking about, and when trouble comes, talk to yourself daily (*peitho*) in faith. Decide to say what God says about you, your situations, and about others. Remember, you serve the God who brings dead things to life! To help you get anchored in this truth, pray this prayer from your heart:

> *Father, thank You that I don't have a pretend faith — I have authentic faith. I curse every negative thought and every doubtful insinuation that is coming against me, in the name of Jesus. Thank You for giving me a divine poker that enables me to stir the fire of Your gift that's in me. I no longer have to be dominated by a spirit of fear. I can speak faith to myself just as Paul did while he was in prison. Help me, Lord, to purposely remember all the ways You have faithfully come through for me and my family, and in doing so, stir the fire of my faith so that it's burning brightly once again. Dominate me by Your divine power, Lord, to stay in place where You've put me and to do what You've called me to do. In Jesus' precious name. Amen!"*

STUDY QUESTIONS

> Study to shew thyself approved unto God, a workman that needeth not to be ashamed, rightly dividing the word of truth.
> — 2 Timothy 2:15

1. What new insights did you learn about Nero's family tree? How about Nero's reign and the great fire of Rome? How do these facts enrich your understanding of what was going on in the Early Church and what they were facing?

2. Are you feeling overwhelmed by what you've been called to do? God promises to provide you with both His *mercy* and His *grace*. Take some time to look up these key verses and write down what the Holy Spirit shows you about God's supernatural provisions of mercy and grace.

    - Titus 3:3-7
    - Micah 7:18,19
    - Lamentations 3:22,23
    - Hebrews 4:15,16
    - 2 Corinthians 9:8; Psalm 84:11
    - James 4:6; 1 Peter 5:5

3. The reason we often become immobilized by fear over our future is because we've forgotten the faithfulness of God in our past. What does Psalm 77:11 and 12 tell us to do to help us refocus on the goodness of God? How might Psalm 100:4 and 5 also be helpful in building your faith?

4. First John 4:18 (*AMPC*) says, "There is no fear in love [dread does not exist], but full-grown (complete, perfect) love turns fear out of doors and expels every trace of terror...." Friend, this is one of your greatest and most powerful weapons against fear — a deeper, more real revelation of God's love! Take some time to really meditate on John 3:16,17; Romans 5:5-8; and First John 4:9-19. Then make Paul's prayer in Ephesians 3:16-19 a personal prayer of your own.

PRACTICAL APPLICATION

> But be ye doers of the word, and not hearers only,
> deceiving your own selves.
> —James 1:22

1. Take a few moments to reflect on the five false allegations Nero brought against First Century Christians. Are you seeing any of these kinds of accusations resurfacing against believers today? If so, in what ways?

2. To help Timothy overcome fear, Paul reminded him of the real, genuine faith that was alive in his grandmother and his mother and that was now living in him. Can you remember who introduced you to Jesus and passed on the faith to you? Was it a family member? A friend? What was it about their life that you admired and desired to see in your own? Who are you passing the faith on to?

3. If someone were to carefully observe your life, would they say you had "unfeigned," genuine faith? Or would they describe you as more of an actor wearing a mask and putting on a show?

4. By your remembering and recalling God's faithfulness to you in times past, you will stir up the gift of God that is in you and defeat fear. Take time to make a list of the many good things God has done in your life. These would include:

   - Times He has shown you MERCY when you didn't deserve it

   - Times He gave you GRACE (power) to do what you couldn't do on your own

   - Times He faithfully protected, provided, directed, and demonstrated His LOVE

   Use this list and add to it often! By remembering and feeding on God's faithfulness to you in the past, you will strengthen your faith in the Lord and defeat the spirit of fear!

5. Can you remember an extremely difficult and dark situation that you felt there was no way out of — yet somehow God delivered you? What was going on, and how did He bring you through it? What did He teach you through that experience that you're grateful to have learned? How does remembering this situation give you hope that God will faithfully bring you through difficulty again?

PART 2

TOPIC
How To Speak Faith to Yourself in Troubled Times

SYNOPSIS

"What triggers a Satanic attack?" Many have asked this question — maybe even you. The Bible gives us one primary reason we are often assaulted by Satan, and it's found in Hebrews 10:32 (*NKJV*), which says, "But recall the former days in which, after you were illuminated, you endured a great struggle with sufferings." Here we see that receiving an illumination — or *revelation* of truth — from God is what often triggers an attack from the enemy.

Realize that when God shows you something new about who He is or who you are in Christ, the devil is not going to simply roll over and play dead. Rather, he's going to counter any advancement you make with a strategic attack to try and stop you. The apostle Paul experienced this firsthand on several occasions, eventually being arrested and imprisoned for a crime he didn't commit.

Yet despite Paul's imprisonment, he wrote a letter of encouragement from his cell to his spiritual son, Timothy, who was struggling with fear. Interestingly, he opened his letter with this greeting: "Paul, an apostle of Jesus Christ by the will of God, according to the promise of life which is in Christ Jesus" (2 Timothy 1:1).

We saw in Part 1 of this study guide that the words "according to" in Greek are a translation of the word *kata*, which describes *something that is dominating, subjugating,* or *conquering*. Considering this meaning, we could translate this verse as saying, "*Paul, an apostle of Jesus Christ, being dominated, being subjugated, being conquered by the promise of life that is in Christ Jesus.*"

Paul made this powerful declaration of faith about his life at a time when the Church was being attacked by a spirit of death on every side. The same is true for us as believers today. We, too, are *dominated, conquered, and subjugated* by the promise of life which is in Christ Jesus — regardless of what is going on around us. With God's help, we can learn how to speak faith to ourselves in troubled times.

The emphasis of this lesson:

As persecution spread to Ephesus, fear began to take a toll on Timothy. Paul reminded him that God has not given him — and us — a spirit of fear, but of power, love, and a sound mind. When we take a stand for what's right, God's power will join itself to us. Like Paul, we must talk to ourselves when we're in trouble, reminding ourselves of who God is, what He's done, and how He's well able to preserve and protect our lives. If we'll get a grip on our mouth and speak words of faith and not fear, the attack will pass, and we'll remain in victory.

Nero's Nuttiness Came Naturally

Paul's imprisonment and the widespread persecution of the Church started under the reign of Emperor Nero. A careful review of Nero's crazy family helps us understand how nuttiness came naturally to him. For example, his great-great-grandfather was Julius Caesar, and his great-grandfather was Caesar Augustus — the first Roman Emperor who ruled for 56 years and declared himself to be God.

When Caesar Augustus' reign ended, the throne went to his nephew and adopted son Tiberias, who was a sexual pervert. He ruled for about 22 years, and during his reign, he eventually left the city of Rome and went to live on the isle of Capri, which he called "Pleasure Island." He was so committed to entertaining himself with orgies that he requisitioned sexual activities to take place on that island 24 hours a day. Tiberius ruled the Roman Empire from Capri for 14 years.

On the isle of Capri with Tiberius was his nephew, Caligula, who was mistreated sexually by his uncle and by other men for nearly 14 years. When Tiberius died, Caligula came to power and ruled the empire for about 4 years, bringing to the throne with him all the mental, emotional, and sexual abuse by his uncle. Like his great-uncle Caesar Augustus, Caligula also believed himself to be God. He was so wicked that his own military murdered him.

When Caligula died, the throne went to his uncle, whose name was Claudius. He was married to a woman named Agrippina, and Agrippina was the sister of Caligula. At some point during Caligula's life, he had an incestuous relationship with Agrippina, so when she became the emperor's wife, all the woundedness in her soul was carried to the throne.

What's interesting is that Claudius had a son named Britannicus from a previous marriage. Legally, when Claudius died, Britannicus was to take the throne. However, his wife, Agrippina, also had a son from a previous marriage whose name was Nero, and she wanted Nero to be the next Emperor of Rome. Being the conniver that she was, history tells us that to bring about her wish, Agrippina fed her husband, Emperor Claudius, a bowl of poisonous mushrooms. Shortly after he died, she proclaimed that her son Nero was the new emperor of the Roman Empire.

Egotism and Delusion Dominated Nero's Life

In Nero's formative years, his mother, Agrippina, had repeatedly told him that he was God and could do anything he wanted and that nothing he did was wrong. At age 16, he was thrust to the throne. Surprisingly, for the first five years of his reign, Nero was a seemingly good emperor, celebrated and loved by the low-class commoners. But when those "golden years" were finished, Nero grew tired of being told what to do and began killing anyone who opposed him.

Two of the first people he eliminated were his teachers Seneca the Younger and Lucius Annaeus. Their deaths were followed by the killing of certain members of the Roman Senate, and when Nero could no longer tolerate the scheming and manipulation of his mother, he had Agrippina killed as well, which seemed to cause a sudden snap in Nero's thinking.

Now believing himself to be God, Nero felt free to do anything he wanted or dreamed. Blinded by pride, he was convinced that he was the greatest artist, musician, singer, and actor. Although performing publicly was not permissible for emperors, Nero took to the stage to act and sing, and his murderous ways accompanied him. In fact, people were so terrified of what Nero would do, it is documented that a pregnant woman who attended one of his concerts actually gave birth to her child during his performance for fear of being killed if she left.

Not only did Nero believe he was the best performer but also the greatest architect that ever lived. He planned on tearing down the ancient city of Rome and building a brand-new city in its place, calling it "Neropolis." In the middle of the new city would sit his new, 300-acre home, which he called "The Golden Palace." The entire exterior of the house was to be completely veneered in mother-of-pearl, which was then to be covered with gold leaf; hence, the name "The Golden Palace."

When Nero went to the Roman Senate and asked for permission to tear down one of the most historic sections of Rome to build his palace, they said no. "You may think you're God," they basically said, "but we're not going to let you tear down *our houses* for you to build your palace."

Naturally, Nero did not take no for an answer, so he returned to his palace just outside of Rome and met with a group of his servants. "Start a fire in Circus Maximus," he ordered, "and do it when people are away and unable to put it out." His servants obeyed him, and the fire soon engulfed the entire city. After seven days, the blaze had destroyed 3 of the 14 major sections of Rome, the sections that just happened to be where Nero wanted to build his palace.

When the construction of Nero's 300-acre home got underway, the news began to circulate throughout the city of Rome that it was Nero who had instigated the fire. For that reason, the Roman Senate summoned him to stand trial for his actions with the possibility of execution if convicted. When the day came for him to appear before the Senate, he came prepared to deliver his greatest theatrical performance of all.

Nero's 'Fake News' Pitted the Roman Empire Against Christians

"How could you think that *I*, Nero, would burn down my beloved city of Rome?" He cried. "I can tell you who did this dastardly deed because my spies have brought me the information."

"Tell us," the Senate responded, "Who burned down the city of Rome?"

"It was those Christians!" Nero sneered. "They're a new sect in our town, and they're the ones who burned down the city of Rome." Nero then brought five allegations against the Christians, which were partially true but taken as a whole were lies.

A Review of the Five False Charges Nero Brought Against Christians:

1. "*Christians are lawbreakers,*" Nero said. "They don't have permission to meet, yet they're meeting in secret underground gatherings." To a degree, that was true, because Roman law said people couldn't

meet as a group unless they had the express approval of the emperor. Since Nero had never given his approval, every time Christians met together, they were breaking Roman law.

But they had to make a choice: obey the law of man or obey the law of God. Although Roman law said they couldn't meet without Rome's permission, the law of God clearly states we are not to forsake the assembling of ourselves together as believers (*see* Hebrews 10:25). So they had to decide which law they were going to obey, and they chose to obey and submit to the *higher* law — God's law. While in man's eyes, they were lawbreakers, in God's eyes they were covenant keepers.

2. "*Christians are talking about another King and another Kingdom,*" Nero added. Of course, they were talking about King Jesus and the Kingdom of God, but Nero made it sound like Christians were rebellious subverters of government. It sounds a lot like what we're dealing with today.

3. "*Christians are sexual perverts,*" Nero exclaimed. "In their illegal gatherings, they practice something called 'the love feast.'" In truth, "the love feast" was not a wild orgy like Nero led the Senate to believe. It was a meal shared by believers before taking communion. The fact that Nero was accusing Christians of being sexually perverse is simply ludicrous. If anyone was sexually twisted it was Nero, who at the time was married to two men.

4. "*Christians are cannibals,*" was Nero's fourth allegation. He told the senate, "Jesus of Nazareth, the leader of their sect, said, 'Except you eat My flesh and drink My blood, you have no part in Me.' And in their illegal meetings, they're eating flesh and drinking blood!" Of course, they were not eating flesh and drinking blood. The practice Nero was describing was communion, but he was so convincing with this charge that the Church had to fight rumors of cannibalism for 200 years after that. Here we see the power of *fake news*.

5. "*Christians are the ones that burned Rome,*" he then claimed. "I don't know how or why you think *I* burned down the city of Rome. Have you not heard what these Christians have been saying on our streets? They've been standing on the corners preaching that in the future, a *huge fire* of judgment is going to come. We should have listened to them because they were giving us a clue that they were going to burn down the city of Rome."

After Nero finished his dramatic presentation, he was so convincing that the Roman Senate believed him, and for the first time in history, governmental persecution was launched against the Church. When we read about persecution in the book of Acts, especially in the earlier years, they are all religious persecutions. The official, governmental persecution against Christians didn't start until 64 AD — about 30 to 40 years after Pentecost. This tyranny took place in all the major cities of the Roman Empire, including Rome, Alexandria, Antioch, and Ephesus. Where was Timothy when all this began to take place? He was in the city of Ephesus.

Fear Began To Take a Toll on Timothy and the Church of Ephesus

On Paul's second missionary journey, he met Aquila and Priscilla, and together they began planting churches, and one of those churches was in the city of Ephesus. Many years later, Paul's spiritual son, Timothy, was installed as that church's lead pastor, continuing the work of preaching the Gospel and training new ministers to fill positions across the continent of Asia.

When persecution reached Ephesus, many believers left the church — people Timothy thought would always faithfully serve by his side. Those fiery trials began to reveal the true quality of people's faith and their level of commitment to Christ. As thousands were walking out of the church and abandoning Timothy, a tsunami of discouragement and fear came crashing down on him.

What made matters worse was the fact that Timothy was the most visible leader in the city of Ephesus. As such, he knew that at any moment there could be a knock at his own door, and he would be arrested for his faith. He also knew if the Romans arrested him, they would likely make his death as horrific as possible to strike terror into the hearts of believers and scare them out of their faith.

Timothy was so taken by a spirit of fear that he wrote a letter to Paul asking him for help. Where was Paul when he received Timothy's letter? He was locked up in prison in the city of Rome, awaiting execution for a crime he didn't commit. Apparently, when the Roman militia rounded up all the Christians for allegedly setting fire to Rome, Paul was also arrested and charged as one of the chief arsonists. As news of his capture circulated the city, Paul sat in seclusion, unable to defend himself.

Although we don't know exactly what Timothy wrote, we do know that he must have been sobbing bitterly as he penned his letter. Scholars believe that when Paul received the letter, he could see the stains of Timothy's teardrops on the parchment. That is why Paul said he was "…mindful of thy [Timothy's] tears" (2 Timothy 1:4).

God Has Not Given Us a Spirit of Fear!

Under the inspiration of the Holy Spirit, Paul told Timothy, "For God hath not given us the spirit of fear; but of power, and of love, and of a sound mind" (2 Timothy 1:7). As we noted in Part 1, **fear is a spirit**, and you can feel its effects when it comes in the room. It brings anxiety, worry, panic, and dread with it. In this verse, the word "fear" is the Greek word *deilia*, which means *timidity, fearfulness*, or *cowardice*. It describes *something that causes you to retreat* or *something that causes you to feel the need to protect yourself*. Instead of moving forward in faith and taking new territory, Timothy was retreating into himself and hiding because fear had a hold of him. To jolt him back into the truth, Paul told him, "God has not given you the spirit of cowardice, Timothy, that causes you to retreat and hide; but He has given you a spirit of power, love, and a sound mind."

We have been given power. The word "power" in the Greek here is *dunamis*, and while it does describe *explosive power* and is where we get the word *dynamite*, it is also the very word used to describe *a force of nature*, like *a hurricane, a tornado*, or *an earthquake*. This tells us that when the power of God is operating inside us, we are like a spiritual earthquake that effectively shakes things up, or like a spiritual hurricane or spiritual tornado that blows things out of the way.

Furthermore, the word *dunamis* — translated here as "power" — is the same word that was used mostly by the Roman Empire to describe *the full might of an advancing army*. Paul's use of this term indicates that when the power of God is operating in you, you become the equivalent of a one-man army with the ability to move forward and to push back darkness.

But remember, if you have a spirit of fear operating in you like Timothy did, you cannot operate in power, you cannot walk in love, and you cannot function with a sound mind. Rather than move forward in power, a spirit of fear paralyzes you and eventually forces you into retreat mode. That's where Timothy was at the time of this letter. He was wounded by the people who had abandoned him, and although he needed to choose new leaders to replace those who had walked out, he was so seized with fear that he was struggling to trust people again. That's why in the second chapter, Paul told him how to choose the next group of leaders (*see* 2 Timothy 2:2).

We have also been given a sound mind. The phrase "sound mind" in Second Timothy 1:7 is taken from the Greek word *sophroneo*, which is a compound of the words *sodzo* and *phroneo*. The word *sodzo* means *to save* or *to deliver*, and the word *phroneo* carries the idea of a person's *intelligence* or *total frame of thinking* — including one's *emotions, rationale*, and *logic*. When compounded, these two words form the word *sophronismos* — translated "sound mind" — and it describes *a mind that has been delivered, rescued, revived, salvaged, and protected and is now safe and set free of all inhibitions.*

When you give place to a spirit of fear, you have an *unsound* mind like Timothy did. It is a mind that is irrational and imagines all the worse-case-scenarios that could happen — most of which could never happen. If your mind is being bombarded by fear and you're tempted to give in to it, take time to allow God's Word and the Holy Spirit to work in you to deliver, rescue, revive, and salvage your mind!

When We Take a Stand for What's Right, God's Power Joins Itself to Us

Paul went on to say, "Be not thou therefore ashamed of the testimony of our Lord, nor of me his prisoner: but be thou partaker of the afflictions of the gospel according to the power of God" (2 Timothy 1:8). This verse shows us the extent to which the spirit of fear had begun to control Timothy. He had become so afflicted by fear that he was tempted to be "ashamed of the testimony of the Lord" and ashamed of Paul, his spiritual father, who was in prison and charged as one of the chief arsonists. Fear was speaking to Timothy, telling him if he remained in relationship with Paul, it could cost him his life.

Therefore, Paul urged him, "Be not thou therefore ashamed of the testimony of our Lord, nor of me his prisoner…" (2 Timothy 1:8). What's interesting is that when we read this in the Greek text, the structure is a double negative with a prohibition. That means we could translate this part of the verse as Paul saying, "Stop it! Stop it now. Stop being ashamed of the testimony of the Lord, and stop being ashamed of me, His prisoner.…"

Then Paul said, "...But be thou partaker of the afflictions of the gospel according to the power of God" (2 Timothy 1:8). Paul was not wishing afflictions on anyone, including Timothy. Nevertheless, when you take a stand for what is right in a world that celebrates wrong, sometimes you will have to deal with the negative repercussions.

The good news is that if you'll stand your ground and not budge from your position of what's right, God will show up and empower you! The phrase "according to" here is a translation of the same Greek word we saw in Second Timothy 1:1 — the word *kata*, which describes *one who is being dominated, conquered, and subjugated* by the power of God. To put it plainly, if you will take a stand for what is right, God's power will join itself to you, and even though you're in the midst of a difficult situation, you will be dominated, conquered, and subjugated by the power of God that has come to strengthen and empower you in the midst of your stand.

Jesus Has Abolished Death

In the next few verses, the apostle Paul began to explain to Timothy — and us — about the glorious gift of salvation God has provided. He said, "[God] who hath saved us, and called us with an holy calling, not according to our works, but according to his own purpose and grace, which was given us in Christ Jesus before the world began, but is now made manifest by the appearing of our Saviour Jesus Christ, who hath abolished death, and hath brought life and immortality to light through the gospel" (2 Timothy 1:9,10).

The fact that Jesus has "abolished death" was a very pertinent message at that moment. As news of Roman persecution reached the ears of believers at the church of Ephesus, a spirit of fear of death was sent out to gain and maintain a chokehold on believers — including Timothy. Thus, Timothy needed to know and believe that Jesus had conquered death and offered new life. And we need to know and believe this too!

Like Paul, the Cause of Our Suffering Is Often God's Call on Our Lives

Paul went on to say, "Whereunto I am appointed a preacher, and an apostle, and a teacher of the Gentiles" (2 Timothy 1:11). The word "whereunto" refers to the previous two verses and points to the glorious Gospel of Jesus Christ. Essentially, when Paul said, "I am appointed to be a preacher, an apostle, and a teacher of the Gospel to the Gentiles," he was explaining and magnifying his calling.

Then in verse 12, Paul said, "For the which cause I also suffer these things…" (2 Timothy 1:12). For what cause was Paul suffering? He was suffering because he had been appointed to be a preacher, an apostle, and a teacher of the Gospel to the Gentiles. How was he suffering? He had been arrested on false charges and confined to prison until his sentence of death was carried out.

According to Second Timothy 4:16 and 17, Paul had already been on trial once. He said, "At my first answer no man stood with me, but all men forsook me: I pray God that it may not be laid to their charge. Notwithstanding the Lord stood with me, and strengthened me; that by me the preaching might be fully known, and that all the Gentiles might hear: and I was delivered out of the mouth of the lion."

From this passage, we can see that Paul knew what it felt like to be abandoned, and this wasn't his first time. He told Timothy earlier in his letter "…that all they which are in Asia be turned away from me; of whom are Phygellus and Hermogenes" (2 Timothy 1:15). What's so alarming about this verse is that 90 percent of Paul's ministry took place in Asia. Yet, as he was sitting in a Roman prison for supposedly starting a fire that burned down Rome, most of the people he worked with in Asia wouldn't come and speak a single word in his defense. Clearly, Paul knew much more about abandonment than Timothy, but Paul was able to separate what was happening to him and minister to his young apprentice in the faith.

Paul knew he wasn't fighting against human beings made of flesh and blood (*see* Ephesians 6:12). He was fighting against unseen, evil spirits that were coming after the call of God on his life. This is what he described in Second Timothy 1:11 and 12, where he said, "Whereunto I am appointed a preacher, and an apostle, and a teacher of the Gentiles. For the which cause I also suffer these things…." Paul's calling was the real cause of his suffering — not the charge of arson.

It's interesting to note that the word "suffer" in verse 12 is the Greek word *pasho*, which means *to physically suffer* or *emotionally suffer*. It can also describe *strong feelings*. At that moment, Paul was having to mentally and emotionally deal with the fact that the people he loved and had poured so much into had abandoned him when he really needed help. He was also trying to come to grips with the fact that his name was now legendary throughout Rome for all the wrong reasons.

Rather Than Being Ashamed or Embarrassed Paul Was 'Persuaded' by God's Faithfulness

Immediately after Paul identified the call of God on His life as the reason he was suffering mental and emotional anguish, he went on to make this remarkable declaration:

> **…Nevertheless I am not ashamed: for I know whom I have believed, and am persuaded that he is able to keep that which I have committed unto him against that day.**
> — 2 Timothy 1:12

There are several key words in this verse, and the first one is the word "ashamed." It is the Greek word *epaishunomai*, which means *to be disgraced, put to shame, embarrassed*, or *to be red-faced*. Despite everything that was being said about Paul, he was not disgraced or embarrassed. He knew who he was and who he was not. Even though he was in prison, he was not ashamed. Why? He said, "…For I know whom I have believed…" (2 Timothy 1:12).

The phrase "I know" is a translation of the Greek word *oida*, which means *to see, perceive, understand, or comprehend*. It describes *knowledge gained by personal experience* or *personal observation*. This word was the equivalent of Paul saying, "I've had a great deal of experience with Jesus and personally observed His power in my life." As a result of this knowing, Paul said, "…[I] am persuaded that he is able…" (2 Timothy 1:12).

The word "persuaded" here is the Greek word *peitho*, and it describes *one who is convinced, coaxed, or swayed from one opinion to the opinion held by another*. This is a person who has *absolute confidence* and is *convinced to the core* with *rock-solid certainty*. The use of this word *peitho*, translated here as "persuaded," tells us that while Paul was suffering in prison, he had moments when he may have been tempted to be fearful about his future because it didn't look good. Therefore, he did a lot of *self-talk*. That's what this word *peitho* can describe — *self-persuasion*. If all he did was focus on the abandonment and rejection of others, he, too, would have been taken captive by a spirit of fear.

When you're in trouble and find yourself in a place of isolation and have no one else to encourage you, you need to speak to yourself and remind yourself of who God is and what He's done in your life. Paul began to speak out in the right way, pushing back against the devil's lies and turning a deaf ear to his emotions. In that dark, dank prison, he coaxed and convinced himself that God was "…able to keep that which [he had] committed unto him against that day" (2 Timothy 1:12).

God Is 'Able To Keep' Us!

When Paul said, "God is able," the word "able" is the Greek word *dunatos*, and it describes *ability, power,* or *a powerful force.* It denotes *amazing ability* and means *to be able, capable,* or *competent for any task.* Paul's use of this word demonstrates his belief that God is *a force that was well-able or capable and competent* to "keep" him.

This word "keep" in Greek is *phulasso*, and it means *to save, protect, preserve,* or *guard*. It describes *a military guard who shows uninterrupted vigilance in guarding territory*. It is also the word used to depict *the uninterrupted vigilance shepherds show in keeping their flocks*. Paul's use of the word *phulasso* (keep), was the equivalent of him saying, "I am the Lord's property, and as my Great Soldier, He is standing guard over me with uninterrupted vigilance. Likewise, He is also my Great Shepherd and is watching over my life with uninterrupted vigilance."

Thus, Paul said, "I am totally convinced that God is fully competent to guard, protect, and preserve what I have committed unto him against that day." The word "committed" in Second Timothy 1:12 is the Greek word *paratheke*, a compound of the word *para* and a form of the word *tithemi*. The word *para* means *alongside*, and the word *tithemi* means *to place* or *to position*. When these two words come together to form *paratheke*, it carries the idea of *pulling up alongside something and making a deposit*; or *committing into one's charge or trust for safekeeping*.

A great example of this word *paratheke* — "committed" — is the act of making a night deposit at a bank. Usually somewhere on the bank building is a large, metal door that is connected to a safety deposit container in the bank. To make a deposit, you would pull up alongside the thick metal door, pull it down, and slip your envelope into the small horizontal opening. Once the door is pushed closed, the deposit is safely secured inside the bank and cannot be touched or tampered with in any way.

In the same way, when you give your life to Christ, you come alongside Him and *deposit* yourself *into Him* and out of the enemy's reach. In that moment, you are safe *in Christ*, and nothing and no one can tamper with or touch you. That is what the apostle Paul was saying — and he was making this declaration of faith from a Roman prison cell, of all places. He believed beyond a shadow of a doubt that God was able to keep him until "that day," which refers to the day we see Jesus face-to-face and our mission here is completed.

It Was Paul's Position of Great Influence That Caused Him To Be Attacked

In addition to receiving divine revelation from God, there is something else that triggers a satanic attack. Paul talked about it in Second Corinthians 12:7, which says, "And lest I should be exalted above measure through the abundance of the revelations, there was given to me a thorn in the flesh, the messenger of Satan to buffet me, lest I should be exalted above measure."

There have been several interpretations as to what Paul is saying here. Some have said that he had a problem with pride because of the revelations God gave him, so God assigned the devil to keep him humble. But since pride began with the devil, it seems that if the devil had been assigned to Paul, he would have made the issue of pride worse in Paul's life.

One of the keys to understanding the meaning of this verse is found in the phrase "exalted above measure." It is a translation of the Greek word *huperairo*, a compound of the words *huper* and *airo*. The word *huper* means *over, above, and beyond* and depicts *something that is way beyond measure*. It conveys the idea of something that is *greater, superior, higher, better, more than a match for, utmost, paramount,* or *foremost*. It describes something that is *first-rate, first-class, top-notch, unsurpassed, unequaled, and unrivaled by any person or thing*. The second part of the word *huperairo* is *airo*, which means *to lift up, to raise,* or *to be exalted*.

When the words *huper* and *airo* are compounded to form *huperairo*, it depicts *a person who has been supremely exalted* or *one who has been magnified, increased, and lifted up to a place of great influence*. With this understanding, we can see that Paul was saying, "As a result of the abundance of revelations God has given me, I have been raised to a position of great influence...."

The word "abundance" in Second Corinthians 12:7 is the Greek word *huperballo*, and it describes *something excessive* or *way over the top*. It is the very word that was used to describe *an archer who pulled back on his bow to shoot an arrow, but he shot way, way, way over the top of the goal*. By using this word, Paul is telling us that the kinds of divine revelation he received were way over the top of something ordinary.

What Was Paul's 'Thorn in the Flesh'?

It was because of these extraordinary, over-the-top revelations that Paul said, "...there was given to me a thorn in the flesh, the messenger of Satan to buffet me, lest I should be exalted above measure" (2 Corinthians 12:7).

Paul's *thorn* has been the topic of much discussion in the Church. In Greek, the word "thorn" is *skolops*, which describes *a dangerously sharp, spiked instrument or tool*. What's interesting is this word was also used to describe *the stake on which an enemy's head was stuck after being decapitated*. By using this word *skolops* — translated here as "thorn" — Paul was literally saying, "I am making such advancements with the Gospel and my position has become so exalted and influential that the devil is after me and he wants my head on a stake!"

The fact that Paul said the thorn was *given* to him often causes people to assume that it was given to him by God, but that is not what the verse says. Rather, it says that the thorn in the flesh was "the messenger of Satan." The Greek word for "Satan" is *Satanas*, meaning *one who conspires against*. It was Satan — not God — that had sent out one of his "messengers," and the word "messengers" is the Greek word *angelos*, describing *a messenger who is dispatched on a specific assignment*.

The purpose of the satanic messenger was to "buffet" Paul. The word "buffet" is the Greek word *kolaphidzo*, which is from a word that describes *the fist* or *knuckles*. Here it refers to *beatings with the fist*, and the Greek tense indicates *unending, unrelenting, continuous, repetitious beatings*. This was Paul's "thorn in the flesh" — a demonic attack sent out by Satan himself to relentlessly and continuously beat and attack Paul in order to distract and derail him from his God-ordained purpose.

Taking into account the original Greek meaning of these key words, here is the *Renner Interpretive Version (RIV)* of Second Corinthians 12:7:

> **Because of the phenomenal revelations I have received and on account of the vast number of these revelations that God has entrusted to me — and to hinder the highly visible progress I am making — a special messenger has been sent from Satan to harass me with constant distractions and headaches. There's no doubt about it! Satan wants my head on a stake! Satan is constantly trying to buffet and distract me in an attempt to keep me from reaching a higher level of visibility and recognition and to sidetrack me from preaching my revelations.**

God Enabled Paul To See the Real Reasons He Was Imprisoned

Friend, understand that sometimes it is your spiritual progress and increased level of visibility and influence for God's Kingdom that causes Satan to launch an attack. That is what happened to the apostle Paul.

Around the time that the city of Rome was set on fire, Paul was making unbelievable progress in his ministry. The Church was emerging, and the church of Ephesus had grown explosively. One scholar says it's possible that 50 percent of Ephesus had come to Christ, which would mean about 100,000 people were a part of that church. It was during this tremendous progress that Satan began working through the demented leader Nero to unleash the fire of persecution throughout the Roman Empire, which resulted in Paul's imprisonment.

By the grace of God, Paul recognized the reason for the false charges against him. In essence, what he's saying in Second Timothy 1:11 and 12 is, "You know what? It's not about me. This attack is because I've been appointed a preacher, an apostle, and a teacher to the Gentiles. That's the cause for suffering and why the devil is after what we're doing. Nevertheless, I'm not ashamed or embarrassed. I know who I am and who I'm not, and I know from personal experience who Jesus is. I've been talking to myself, coaxing and convincing myself of the Lord's faithfulness and His unmatched ability to guard and protect my life with uninterrupted vigilance until the day He calls me home."

Remember, "…Faith cometh by hearing, and hearing by the word of God" (Romans 10:17). The original Greek here actually says, "…Faith comes by *hearing* and *hearing* and *hearing* and *hearing*…." If you don't have anyone else to speak positive words of faith to you, speak them to yourself again and again and again. You *will* begin to believe what you repeatedly hear.

To Win the Fight, We Must Get a Grip on Our Lip

Paul went on to instruct Timothy, "Hold fast the form of sound words, which thou hast heard of me, in faith and love which is in Christ Jesus" (2 Timothy 1:13). The words "hold fast" are from the Greek word *echo*, which means *to have, hold, retain,* or *possess*. It carries the idea of *wrapping one's arms around something and refusing to let anyone take it away from you.* Thus, Paul was urging Timothy to hold tightly to and retain possession of "the form of sound words."

In Greek, the word "form" is *hupotoposis*, which is a compound of the words *hupo* and *tupos*. The word *hupo* means *right next to* or *right alongside of*, and the word *tupos* describes *a model* or *pattern*. When *hupo* and *tupos* are compounded to form *hupotoposis*, it means *to stick by the mold or the pattern*. Paul told Timothy to work hard at holding on to the pattern of "sound words" that he had modeled in front of him. The word "sound" here is the Greek word *hugiaino*, and it describes *anything that is wholesome and healthy and that produces a healthy state of being*.

When Paul wrote his second letter to Timothy, they were both being attacked. But while Paul was in faith and fully persuaded of God's keeping power, Timothy was fighting against a spirit of fear. In that moment, Paul told Timothy, "Hold fast the form of sound words, which thou hast heard of me…" (2 Timothy 1:13). In other words, Paul said, "Timothy, stick with and follow the pattern of wholesome, life-giving words, which you've heard from me."

This tells us that Paul had a regular pattern of speaking, and it was so steady and consistent that others, like Timothy, were familiar with it. Basically, Paul was telling Timothy: "When you're tempted to give into fear, get a firm grip on your mouth and watch what you say. Quit just listening to every thought that comes into your mind and start speaking *life-giving* words to yourself. You've seen *me* do it, Timothy. Just do what I'm doing. You have, you hold, and you possess the right pattern of speaking, so stick to it. Make sure you speak words that are going to produce a *healthy* result in your life."

If anyone had the right to speak negative words of anger, fear, and offense, it was Paul. He had been betrayed and abandoned, and he was now in prison. Of all the thousands upon thousands of people he had helped and poured into, not one of them stepped forward to defend him when he was brought to trial (*see* 2 Timothy 4:16). Indeed, everyone in Asia turned away from Paul and walked out on him (*see* 2 Timothy 1:15).

There was one person who came to Paul's aid, and we learn about him in Second Timothy 1:16 and 17, where Paul writes, "The Lord give mercy unto the house of Onesiphorus; for he oft refreshed me, and was not ashamed of my chain: But, when he was in Rome, he sought me out very diligently, and found me." Rather than give in to his emotions and nurture his hurt, Paul kept a grip on his lip and spoke words of faith and love to himself and to his spiritual son Timothy. May God infuse you with His power and desire to tame *your* tongue and speak words of life and health to yourself and others. The rich rewards you will reap are well worth it!

The Need for Healthy Self-Talk

Learning how to talk to oneself is not just an exercise relegated to First Century believers. Christians throughout all generations have had to learn the vital importance of healthy self-talk (*peitho*) during very trying times.

And today — day after day as we watch the news and hear reports of what is going on in the world around us — we have to make a choice as to what we're going to think about, meditate on, and allow to come forth from our lips. If we say everything our mind is thinking, we will eventually "sink our ship"! That is essentially what James 3 tells us:

> **…A tiny rudder makes a huge ship turn wherever the pilot wants it to go, even though the winds are strong. So also the tongue is a small thing, but what enormous damage it can do. A great forest can be set on fire by one tiny spark.**
> **—James 3:4,5 (*TLB*)**

Our tongue is like the rudder of our life, and it will determine where we go and where we don't go. Even in times of trouble, a person's established heart and his unwavering confession of faith will keep the ship of his life on a steady course and will position that individual for all things to work together for his good (*see* Romans 8:28).

With New Opportunities Come New Adversaries — Why Some Attacks Come

Writing to the believers in Corinth, the apostle Paul said, "For a great door and effectual is opened unto me, and there are many adversaries" (1 Corinthians 16:9). Interestingly, in the original Greek, the phrase "opened unto me" describes *a door that swings open by itself.* It's a door that you don't knock on or push open — it just opens in front of you.

With the supernatural opening of that door, the Bible also says, "…And there are *many adversaries*" (1 Corinthians 16:9). Know this: *Adversaries come with progress.* If you feel you've come under attack, you now have a better idea of why the attack has come. But whether it is the result of receiving fresh revelation, an increase in your progress and level of influence, or a divine door opening in your favor, don't let fear take you captive. Grab hold of God's grace and begin to speak faith to yourself!

Paul went on to tell Timothy, "That good thing which was committed unto thee keep by the Holy Ghost which dwelleth in us" (2 Timothy 1:14). It's interesting to note that the word "committed" here is the Greek word *paratheke*, the same word we saw in verse 12. The use of this word tells us that *just like we pulled up alongside Christ and deposited our lives forever into Him, He likewise has pulled alongside us and deposited good things inside us.*

What does God want us to do with what He's deposited in us? He said we are to "keep" it. Here again is a familiar word — the Greek word *phulasso*, which describes *the uninterrupted vigilance of a soldier who watches over an assignment* or *the uninterrupted vigilance of a shepherd watching over his sheep.* So, just as Jesus watches over us, we have been given the task of watching over our assignment and all that He's placed within us. Thankfully, we don't do this in our own strength but by *the power of the Holy Spirit* who dwells in us.

Friend, if you'll hold tight to what is right and stay where God put you, His power will join itself to you — dominating, conquering, and subjugating you. Be mindful to think on what is true, right, and pure (*see* Philippians 4:8), and keep a grip on the words of your lips. Speak what is wholesome and it will produce a healthy state of being. Eventually, the attack will pass, and you will remain standing in victory!

STUDY QUESTIONS

> **Study to shew thyself approved unto God, a workman that needeth not to be ashamed, rightly dividing the word of truth.**
> **— 2 Timothy 2:15**

1. The Bible tells us that *fear is a spirit* (2 Timothy 1:7), and it can take on many forms. Oftentimes, fear attacks us in the form of *anxiety* and *worry*. God took time to pen many powerful promises that will help you defeat these forms of fear. Take a few moments to look them up in a few Bible versions and meditate on them whenever you feel anxiety and worry coming against you. What is the Holy Spirit speaking to you in these passages?

   - Matthew 6:25-34
   - Luke 12:22-34
   - Philippians 4:6-8
   - 1 Peter 5:7

2. *Fear* is something that causes you to *retreat and hide* or makes you *feel the need to protect yourself.* Considering this definition, what specific fear is coming against you right now? Using a Bible concordance or an online search engine, look up and write down scriptures that specifically counter the fear you're fighting against.

3. Words are powerful! Just as God spoke and His words created the universe, your words create the world in which you live. Here's a sampling of scriptures revealing just how powerful your words are. Take some time to look up these verses in a few Bible versions, and then write out and commit to memory the ones that really speak to you.

   - James 3:2-10
   - Proverbs 10:11 and 31; 18:20,21
   - Psalm 34:12,13 and 1 Peter 3:10,11

- Proverbs 13:2,3; 21:23
- James 1:26 and Psalm 19:14; 141:3,4

4. Although there are many kinds of fear that the enemy brings against us, some fears are common to us all. Rather than keep listening to his lies, REPLACE them with the truth of God's Word! Look up and write out these passages, and when the enemy tries to speak his lies, open your mouth and declare truth over your life!

- *Replace* fear of lack with **Faith in God's Provision**
  Psalm 34:9,10; 84:11; 2 Corinthians 9:8; Hebrews 13:5,6

- *Replace* fear of harm with **Faith in God's Protection**
  Psalm 34:7; 91; 121; Isaiah 41:10-16; 43:1,2; John 10:27-30

- *Replace* fear of missing God with **Faith in God's Direction**
  Psalm 23:1-3; 25:8,9,12-14; 32:8; 48:14; 73:24; Isaiah 30:21; John 16:13

- *Replace* fear of not knowing what to say with **Faith in God To Speak Through You**
  Matthew 10:19,20; Mark 13:11; Luke 12:11,12; Isaiah 50:4; 1 Corinthians 2:13

- *Replace* fear of death with **Faith that God Has Abolished Death**
  2 Timothy 1:10; Hebrews 2:14,15; John 11:25,26; 17:2,3

PRACTICAL APPLICATION

> But be ye doers of the word, and not hearers only, deceiving your own selves.
> —James 1:22

1. First Century Christians were forced to make a choice: obey the law of man or obey the law of God. Think about it: What would you do if you were forced to make this choice? How would you respond, and how do you think your family members (spouse/children) would respond? What might you do to prepare yourself and your family in the event this *did* happen? (Consider the stories of supernatural courage in Daniel 3 and 6; and Acts 4.)

2. Prior to this lesson, had you ever heard of Paul's "thorn in the flesh" (*see* 2 Corinthians 12:7)? If so, what did you understand it to mean?

Considering the original Greek meaning of this verse, what was Paul's thorn in the flesh? How does this help you better understand his persistent prayers for help and God's response to him about grace in Second Corinthians 12:8-10?

3. When Paul was in prison and tempted to give in to fear, he began to talk to himself (*peitho*), coaxing and convincing himself that God was able to save, protect, and preserve his life. How do you normally react when you find yourself in difficult or overwhelming circumstances? Do you think and talk about the problem? Or do you think and talk about God's ability to keep you and help you through the problem? What changes do you sense the Holy Spirit is prompting you to make in the way you respond?

4. In this lesson, we learned about three things that trigger an attack from the enemy: (1) when God gives us fresh revelation; (2) when we're making progress and our position of influence has expanded; (3) when a divine door of opportunity is opened to us. If you're being attacked, take a few moments to pray: *Lord, what has happened in my life that has triggered this attack? Please help me to remember Your faithfulness to me in the past and give me the wisdom and strength to stand firm, stay put, and speak life-giving words of faith to myself and others. In Jesus' name. Amen.*

Notes

Notes

Notes

CLAIM YOUR FREE RESOURCE!

As a way of introducing you further to the teaching ministry of Rick Renner, we would like to send you FREE of charge his teaching, "How To Receive a Miraculous Touch From God" on CD or USB format.

In His earthly ministry, Jesus commonly healed *all* who were sick of *all* their diseases. In this profound message, learn about the manifold dimensions of Christ's wisdom, goodness, power, and love toward all humanity who came to Him in faith with their needs.

☑ YES, I want to receive Rick Renner's monthly teaching letter!

Simply scan the QR code to claim this resource or go to:
renner.org/claim-your-free-offer

WITH US!

 renner.org

facebook.com/rickrenner • facebook.com/rennerdenise
youtube.com/rennerministries • youtube.com/deniserenner
instagram.com/rickrrenner • instagram.com/rennerministries_
instagram.com/rennerdenise

www.ingramcontent.com/pod-product-compliance
Lightning Source LLC
Chambersburg PA
CBHW061301040426
42444CB00010B/2469